50 Clean Eating Basic Recipes for Home

By: Kelly Johnson

Table of Contents

- Grilled Chicken Breast with Lemon and Herbs
- Quinoa Salad with Fresh Vegetables
- Baked Salmon with Dill and Lemon
- Stir-Fried Tofu with Mixed Vegetables
- Brown Rice and Black Bean Bowl
- Roasted Brussels Sprouts with Balsamic Glaze
- Sweet Potato and Kale Hash
- Mediterranean Chickpea Salad
- Oven-Roasted Turkey Breast
- Steamed Asparagus with Olive Oil and Garlic
- Cauliflower Rice Stir-Fry
- Greek Yogurt Parfait with Fresh Berries
- Lemon Garlic Shrimp Skewers
- Zucchini Noodles with Pesto Sauce
- Mango Salsa Chicken
- Roasted Vegetable Quinoa Bowl
- Grilled Portobello Mushrooms
- Turkey and Vegetable Lettuce Wraps
- Egg White Omelette with Spinach and Tomatoes
- Cucumber Avocado Salad
- Almond-Crusted Baked Chicken Tenders
- Spinach and Feta Stuffed Chicken Breast
- Lentil and Vegetable Soup
- Lemon Herb Baked Cod
- Roasted Sweet Potato Wedges
- Greek Salad with Feta and Olives
- Baked Eggplant Parmesan
- Shrimp and Broccoli Stir-Fry
- Quinoa-Stuffed Bell Peppers
- Caprese Salad with Fresh Mozzarella
- Baked Chicken Thighs with Rosemary
- Avocado and Black Bean Salsa
- Lemon Basil Grilled Chicken
- Broccoli and Cauliflower Gratin
- Turkey and Vegetable Skewers

- Butternut Squash Soup
- Blueberry and Almond Smoothie
- Roasted Garlic Hummus
- Chickpea and Spinach Curry
- Balsamic Glazed Salmon
- Watermelon and Feta Salad
- Turkey and Quinoa Meatballs
- Spaghetti Squash with Tomato Sauce
- Green Bean Almondine
- Berry Chia Seed Pudding
- Grilled Vegetable Kabobs
- Coconut Flour Banana Pancakes
- Lemon Dijon Grilled Chicken
- Greek Tzatziki Sauce
- Mixed Berry Smoothie Bowl

Grilled Chicken Breast with Lemon and Herbs

Ingredients:

- 4 boneless, skinless chicken breasts
- 2 tablespoons olive oil
- 2 tablespoons fresh lemon juice
- 2 cloves garlic, minced
- 1 teaspoon dried oregano
- 1 teaspoon dried thyme
- 1 teaspoon dried rosemary
- Salt and black pepper, to taste
- Lemon slices (for garnish)
- Fresh parsley, chopped (for garnish)

Instructions:

In a small bowl, whisk together olive oil, fresh lemon juice, minced garlic, dried oregano, dried thyme, dried rosemary, salt, and black pepper. This will be your marinade.

Place the chicken breasts in a large resealable plastic bag or shallow dish.

Pour the marinade over the chicken, making sure each breast is well coated. Seal the bag or cover the dish and refrigerate for at least 30 minutes, allowing the chicken to marinate.

Preheat your grill to medium-high heat.

Remove the chicken from the marinade, letting any excess drip off.

Grill the chicken breasts for approximately 6-8 minutes per side or until the internal temperature reaches 165°F (74°C) and the chicken is cooked through.

While grilling, baste the chicken with any remaining marinade to keep it moist.

Once done, transfer the grilled chicken to a serving platter.

Garnish with lemon slices and chopped fresh parsley.

Serve the Grilled Chicken Breast with Lemon and Herbs alongside your favorite side dishes or a fresh salad.

Enjoy your flavorful and herb-infused grilled chicken!

Quinoa Salad with Fresh Vegetables

Ingredients:

For the Salad:

- 1 cup quinoa, rinsed and drained
- 2 cups water
- 1 cucumber, diced
- 1 bell pepper (any color), diced
- 1 cup cherry tomatoes, halved
- 1/2 red onion, finely chopped
- 1/4 cup fresh parsley, chopped
- 1/4 cup fresh mint, chopped (optional)
- Feta cheese, crumbled (optional)

For the Dressing:

- 1/4 cup extra-virgin olive oil
- 2 tablespoons red wine vinegar
- 1 tablespoon lemon juice
- 1 clove garlic, minced
- 1 teaspoon Dijon mustard
- Salt and black pepper, to taste

Instructions:

In a medium saucepan, combine quinoa and water. Bring to a boil, then reduce heat to low, cover, and simmer for about 15 minutes or until the quinoa is cooked and water is absorbed. Remove from heat and let it cool.

In a large salad bowl, combine the cooked quinoa, diced cucumber, diced bell pepper, cherry tomatoes, chopped red onion, fresh parsley, and mint.

In a small bowl or jar, whisk together the olive oil, red wine vinegar, lemon juice, minced garlic, Dijon mustard, salt, and black pepper to create the dressing.

Pour the dressing over the quinoa and vegetable mixture. Toss everything together until well coated.

If using, sprinkle crumbled Feta cheese on top.

Refrigerate the Quinoa Salad with Fresh Vegetables for at least 30 minutes to allow the flavors to meld.

Before serving, give the salad a gentle toss and adjust the seasoning if needed. Serve chilled as a refreshing and nutritious side dish or a light meal.
Enjoy your delicious and vibrant quinoa salad!

Baked Salmon with Dill and Lemon

Ingredients:

- 4 salmon fillets
- 2 tablespoons olive oil
- 2 tablespoons fresh dill, chopped
- 2 tablespoons fresh lemon juice
- 2 cloves garlic, minced
- Salt and black pepper, to taste
- Lemon slices (for garnish)

Instructions:

Preheat your oven to 400°F (200°C). Line a baking sheet with parchment paper. Place the salmon fillets on the prepared baking sheet.

In a small bowl, mix together olive oil, chopped fresh dill, fresh lemon juice, minced garlic, salt, and black pepper to create the marinade.

Brush the salmon fillets with the dill and lemon marinade, ensuring they are well coated on all sides.

If desired, place a few lemon slices on top of each salmon fillet for extra flavor.

Bake in the preheated oven for about 12-15 minutes, or until the salmon is cooked through and flakes easily with a fork.

If you prefer a crispier top, you can broil the salmon for an additional 2-3 minutes after baking.

Remove the baked salmon from the oven and transfer the fillets to serving plates. Garnish with additional fresh dill and lemon slices.

Serve the Baked Salmon with Dill and Lemon alongside your favorite side dishes, such as roasted vegetables or a green salad.

Enjoy this simple and flavorful baked salmon recipe!

Stir-Fried Tofu with Mixed Vegetables

Ingredients:

For the Stir-Fry:

- 14 oz (400g) firm tofu, pressed and cubed
- 2 tablespoons soy sauce (or tamari for a gluten-free option)
- 1 tablespoon sesame oil
- 1 tablespoon vegetable oil
- 1 tablespoon ginger, minced
- 2 cloves garlic, minced
- 1 cup broccoli florets
- 1 bell pepper, thinly sliced
- 1 carrot, julienned
- 1 cup snap peas, ends trimmed
- 1 cup cabbage, shredded
- Green onions, chopped (for garnish)
- Sesame seeds (for garnish)

For the Sauce:

- 2 tablespoons soy sauce
- 1 tablespoon rice vinegar
- 1 tablespoon maple syrup or agave nectar
- 1 teaspoon cornstarch

Instructions:

In a small bowl, mix together the sauce ingredients: soy sauce, rice vinegar, maple syrup, and cornstarch. Set aside.

Heat vegetable oil in a large wok or skillet over medium-high heat.

Add the cubed tofu to the hot wok and stir-fry until it becomes golden brown on all sides.

Drizzle soy sauce and sesame oil over the tofu, continuing to stir-fry for an additional 2-3 minutes. Remove the tofu from the wok and set it aside.

In the same wok, add a bit more vegetable oil if needed. Sauté minced ginger and garlic until fragrant.

Add broccoli, bell pepper, carrot, snap peas, and shredded cabbage to the wok. Stir-fry the vegetables until they are tender-crisp.

Return the cooked tofu to the wok and pour the prepared sauce over the tofu and vegetables. Toss everything together until well coated.

Cook for an additional 2-3 minutes to allow the sauce to thicken.

Garnish the Stir-Fried Tofu with Mixed Vegetables with chopped green onions and sesame seeds.

Serve the stir-fry over cooked rice, quinoa, or noodles.

Enjoy this delicious and nutritious tofu stir-fry with mixed vegetables!

Brown Rice and Black Bean Bowl

Ingredients:

For the Brown Rice:

- 1 cup brown rice
- 2 cups water
- 1/2 teaspoon salt

For the Black Beans:

- 1 can (15 oz) black beans, drained and rinsed
- 1 tablespoon olive oil
- 1 teaspoon ground cumin
- 1 teaspoon chili powder
- 1/2 teaspoon garlic powder
- Salt and black pepper, to taste

For the Bowl:

- Avocado, sliced
- Cherry tomatoes, halved
- Corn kernels (fresh or frozen, thawed)
- Red onion, finely diced
- Fresh cilantro, chopped
- Lime wedges (for serving)
- Optional toppings: salsa, Greek yogurt, shredded cheese

Instructions:

Cook the Brown Rice:
- In a medium saucepan, combine brown rice, water, and salt.
- Bring to a boil, then reduce heat to low, cover, and simmer for about 45-50 minutes or until the rice is cooked and water is absorbed.
- Fluff the rice with a fork and set aside.

Prepare the Black Beans:
- In a skillet, heat olive oil over medium heat.
- Add black beans, ground cumin, chili powder, garlic powder, salt, and black pepper.

- Stir and cook for 5-7 minutes until the beans are heated through and well-seasoned.

Assemble the Bowl:
- Divide the cooked brown rice among serving bowls.
- Top with the seasoned black beans.

Add Your Favorite Toppings:
- Arrange sliced avocado, halved cherry tomatoes, corn kernels, diced red onion, and chopped cilantro on top of the rice and beans.

Optional Toppings:
- Add a dollop of Greek yogurt, a spoonful of salsa, or a sprinkle of shredded cheese if desired.

Serve the Brown Rice and Black Bean Bowl with lime wedges on the side.

Mix everything together before eating and squeeze fresh lime juice over the bowl for extra flavor.

Enjoy this wholesome and satisfying brown rice and black bean bowl!

Roasted Brussels Sprouts with Balsamic Glaze

Ingredients:

- 1 lb Brussels sprouts, trimmed and halved
- 2 tablespoons olive oil
- Salt and black pepper, to taste
- 2 tablespoons balsamic vinegar
- 1 tablespoon honey or maple syrup (optional)
- 1-2 cloves garlic, minced (optional)
- Crushed red pepper flakes (optional, for a hint of spice)

Instructions:

Preheat your oven to 400°F (200°C). Line a baking sheet with parchment paper.
In a large bowl, toss the halved Brussels sprouts with olive oil, salt, and black pepper until they are well coated.
Spread the Brussels sprouts evenly on the prepared baking sheet.
Roast in the preheated oven for 20-25 minutes or until the Brussels sprouts are golden brown and crispy on the edges. Stir halfway through the cooking time for even roasting.
While the Brussels sprouts are roasting, prepare the balsamic glaze. In a small saucepan over medium heat, combine balsamic vinegar, honey or maple syrup (if using), minced garlic (if using), and optional red pepper flakes. Bring the mixture to a simmer and cook for 5-7 minutes, or until it has thickened slightly.
Once the Brussels sprouts are done roasting, transfer them to a serving dish.
Drizzle the balsamic glaze over the roasted Brussels sprouts and toss gently to coat them evenly.
Serve the Roasted Brussels Sprouts with Balsamic Glaze as a delicious side dish for any meal.
Enjoy the caramelized flavor and rich balsamic glaze of this tasty Brussels sprouts dish!

Sweet Potato and Kale Hash

Ingredients:

- 2 medium sweet potatoes, peeled and diced
- 2 tablespoons olive oil
- 1 onion, finely chopped
- 2 cloves garlic, minced
- 1 bunch kale, stems removed and leaves chopped
- Salt and black pepper, to taste
- 1/2 teaspoon smoked paprika (optional)
- 1/4 teaspoon red pepper flakes (optional)
- Poached or fried eggs (optional, for serving)

Instructions:

In a large skillet or frying pan, heat olive oil over medium heat.
Add the diced sweet potatoes to the skillet and cook for about 10-12 minutes, or until they are tender and slightly crispy on the edges. Stir occasionally to ensure even cooking.
Add finely chopped onion to the sweet potatoes and sauté for 2-3 minutes, or until the onion becomes translucent.
Stir in minced garlic and cook for an additional 1 minute until fragrant.
Add chopped kale to the skillet, tossing everything together. Cook for about 3-5 minutes or until the kale is wilted and tender.
Season the Sweet Potato and Kale Hash with salt, black pepper, smoked paprika (if using), and red pepper flakes (if using). Adjust the seasoning to your taste.
If desired, serve the hash with poached or fried eggs on top.
Spoon the Sweet Potato and Kale Hash onto plates or into bowls.
Enjoy this nutritious and flavorful sweet potato and kale hash as a hearty breakfast or a satisfying side dish!

Mediterranean Chickpea Salad

Ingredients:

For the Salad:

- 2 cans (15 oz each) chickpeas, drained and rinsed
- 1 cucumber, diced
- 1 cup cherry tomatoes, halved
- 1 red bell pepper, diced
- 1/2 red onion, finely chopped
- 1/2 cup Kalamata olives, sliced
- 1/2 cup crumbled feta cheese (optional)
- Fresh parsley, chopped (for garnish)

For the Dressing:

- 1/4 cup extra-virgin olive oil
- 2 tablespoons red wine vinegar
- 1 teaspoon dried oregano
- 1 teaspoon dried basil
- 1 clove garlic, minced
- Salt and black pepper, to taste

Instructions:

In a large salad bowl, combine chickpeas, diced cucumber, cherry tomatoes, diced red bell pepper, finely chopped red onion, sliced Kalamata olives, and crumbled feta cheese (if using).
In a small bowl or jar, whisk together the dressing ingredients: olive oil, red wine vinegar, dried oregano, dried basil, minced garlic, salt, and black pepper.
Pour the dressing over the chickpea salad and toss everything together until well coated.
Let the Mediterranean Chickpea Salad sit for at least 15-20 minutes to allow the flavors to meld.
Before serving, garnish the salad with fresh chopped parsley.

Serve the salad as a refreshing side dish, light lunch, or a colorful addition to your Mediterranean-inspired meals.

Enjoy this flavorful and protein-packed chickpea salad!

Oven-Roasted Turkey Breast

Ingredients:

- 1 whole turkey breast (bone-in or boneless), about 3-4 pounds
- 2 tablespoons olive oil
- 1 teaspoon dried thyme
- 1 teaspoon dried rosemary
- 1 teaspoon dried sage
- 1 teaspoon garlic powder
- 1 teaspoon onion powder
- Salt and black pepper, to taste

Instructions:

Preheat your oven to 325°F (163°C).
In a small bowl, mix together the olive oil, dried thyme, dried rosemary, dried sage, garlic powder, onion powder, salt, and black pepper to create a herb-infused rub.
Pat the turkey breast dry with paper towels. If the turkey breast has skin, make sure to loosen it slightly from the meat without removing it.
Rub the herb mixture evenly over the entire surface of the turkey breast, including under the skin if applicable.
Place the turkey breast on a rack in a roasting pan, breast side up.
Roast the turkey breast in the preheated oven. The cooking time will depend on the size of the turkey breast. As a general guideline, roast for about 20 minutes per pound, or until the internal temperature reaches 165°F (74°C).
Baste the turkey breast with pan juices every 30 minutes to keep it moist.
If the skin starts to brown too quickly, you can cover the turkey loosely with aluminum foil.
Once the turkey breast reaches the desired temperature, remove it from the oven and let it rest for about 15-20 minutes before carving.
Carve the Oven-Roasted Turkey Breast into slices and serve with your favorite side dishes.
Enjoy the succulent and herb-infused flavors of this oven-roasted turkey breast!

Steamed Asparagus with Olive Oil and Garlic

Ingredients:

- 1 bunch fresh asparagus
- 2 tablespoons olive oil
- 2 cloves garlic, minced
- Salt and black pepper, to taste
- Lemon wedges (for serving)

Instructions:

Wash and trim the tough ends from the asparagus spears.
In a steamer basket over a pot of simmering water, steam the asparagus for 3-5 minutes or until they are tender-crisp. The cooking time may vary depending on the thickness of the asparagus.
While the asparagus is steaming, heat olive oil in a small pan over medium heat.
Add minced garlic to the pan and sauté for 1-2 minutes, or until the garlic becomes fragrant. Be careful not to let it brown.
Once the asparagus is done steaming, transfer them to a serving plate.
Drizzle the olive oil and garlic mixture over the steamed asparagus.
Season with salt and black pepper to taste.
Garnish with lemon wedges for squeezing over the asparagus before serving.
Toss the asparagus gently to ensure they are coated with the olive oil and garlic.
Serve the Steamed Asparagus with Olive Oil and Garlic as a flavorful and nutritious side dish.
Enjoy the fresh and vibrant taste of this simple steamed asparagus recipe!

Cauliflower Rice Stir-Fry

Ingredients:

- 1 medium head cauliflower, grated or processed into rice-sized pieces
- 2 tablespoons vegetable oil
- 1 onion, finely chopped
- 2 carrots, diced
- 1 bell pepper (any color), diced
- 1 cup broccoli florets
- 2 cloves garlic, minced
- 1/4 cup soy sauce (or tamari for a gluten-free option)
- 1 tablespoon sesame oil
- 1 tablespoon rice vinegar
- 1 teaspoon ginger, grated
- 2 green onions, chopped (for garnish)
- Sesame seeds (for garnish)

Instructions:

Using a box grater or a food processor, grate the cauliflower into rice-sized pieces.
In a large wok or skillet, heat vegetable oil over medium-high heat.
Add finely chopped onion to the hot wok and sauté for 2-3 minutes until the onion becomes translucent.
Add diced carrots, diced bell pepper, and broccoli florets to the wok. Stir-fry for 5-7 minutes, or until the vegetables are tender-crisp.
Push the vegetables to one side of the wok, creating a space in the center.
Add minced garlic to the center and sauté for about 30 seconds until fragrant.
Incorporate the grated cauliflower into the wok and mix it with the vegetables.
In a small bowl, whisk together soy sauce, sesame oil, rice vinegar, and grated ginger to create the sauce.
Pour the sauce over the cauliflower and vegetable mixture. Stir everything together until well coated.
Cook for an additional 3-5 minutes, or until the cauliflower is cooked but still has a slight crunch.
Garnish the Cauliflower Rice Stir-Fry with chopped green onions and sesame seeds.
Serve hot as a flavorful and low-carb alternative to traditional stir-fried rice.

Enjoy this healthy and delicious cauliflower rice stir-fry!

Greek Yogurt Parfait with Fresh Berries

Ingredients:

- 1 cup Greek yogurt
- 1 tablespoon honey or maple syrup
- 1/2 teaspoon vanilla extract
- 1 cup mixed fresh berries (strawberries, blueberries, raspberries)
- Granola (optional, for topping)
- Mint leaves (for garnish)

Instructions:

In a bowl, mix Greek yogurt with honey or maple syrup and vanilla extract. Stir until well combined.

In serving glasses or bowls, layer the Greek yogurt mixture with fresh berries.

Repeat the layering process until you reach the top of the glass or bowl.

Top the parfait with a dollop of Greek yogurt, a drizzle of honey or maple syrup, and a sprinkle of granola if desired.

Garnish with mint leaves for a fresh touch.

Serve the Greek Yogurt Parfait with Fresh Berries immediately as a delicious and nutritious breakfast or dessert.

Enjoy the creamy yogurt, sweet berries, and crunchy granola in every delightful bite!

Lemon Garlic Shrimp Skewers

Ingredients:

- 1 lb large shrimp, peeled and deveined
- 3 tablespoons olive oil
- 3 cloves garlic, minced
- Zest of 1 lemon
- Juice of 1 lemon
- 1 teaspoon dried oregano
- Salt and black pepper, to taste
- Fresh parsley, chopped (for garnish)
- Lemon wedges (for serving)

Instructions:

In a bowl, mix together olive oil, minced garlic, lemon zest, lemon juice, dried oregano, salt, and black pepper to create the marinade.
Add the peeled and deveined shrimp to the bowl, ensuring they are well coated with the marinade. Let them marinate for at least 15-20 minutes in the refrigerator.
Preheat your grill or grill pan over medium-high heat.
Thread the marinated shrimp onto skewers, ensuring they are evenly distributed.
Grill the shrimp skewers for 2-3 minutes per side or until they turn opaque and develop a slight char.
Remove the shrimp skewers from the grill and place them on a serving plate.
Garnish the Lemon Garlic Shrimp Skewers with chopped fresh parsley.
Serve with lemon wedges on the side for squeezing over the shrimp before eating.
Enjoy these flavorful and zesty lemon garlic shrimp skewers as a tasty appetizer or a main dish!

Zucchini Noodles with Pesto Sauce

Ingredients:

For the Pesto Sauce:

- 2 cups fresh basil leaves, packed
- 1/2 cup grated Parmesan cheese
- 1/2 cup pine nuts or walnuts
- 3 cloves garlic, peeled
- 1/2 cup extra-virgin olive oil
- Salt and black pepper, to taste
- 1 tablespoon lemon juice (optional)

For the Zucchini Noodles:

- 4 medium zucchini, spiralized into noodles
- 1 tablespoon olive oil
- Cherry tomatoes, halved (for garnish)
- Extra grated Parmesan cheese (for garnish)

Instructions:

Prepare the Pesto Sauce:
- In a food processor, combine fresh basil, grated Parmesan cheese, pine nuts or walnuts, and peeled garlic cloves.
- Pulse until the ingredients are finely chopped.
- With the food processor running, slowly drizzle in the olive oil until the pesto reaches your desired consistency.
- Season with salt and black pepper to taste. Add lemon juice if desired for a citrusy kick.

Cook the Zucchini Noodles:
- In a large skillet, heat olive oil over medium heat.
- Add the spiralized zucchini noodles to the skillet and sauté for 2-3 minutes or until they are just tender but still have a slight crunch.
- Remove excess moisture from the noodles if needed by patting them with a paper towel.

Toss with Pesto Sauce:
- Add a generous amount of pesto sauce to the zucchini noodles. Toss everything together until the noodles are well coated with the pesto.

Garnish and Serve:
- Transfer the Zucchini Noodles with Pesto Sauce to serving plates.
- Garnish with halved cherry tomatoes and extra grated Parmesan cheese.

Serve immediately and enjoy this light and flavorful zucchini noodle dish!

Note: You can also customize the dish by adding grilled chicken, shrimp, or your favorite protein for extra protein and texture.

Mango Salsa Chicken

Ingredients:

For the Mango Salsa:

- 1 ripe mango, peeled, pitted, and diced
- 1/2 red onion, finely chopped
- 1 red bell pepper, diced
- 1 jalapeño, seeds removed and finely chopped
- 1/4 cup fresh cilantro, chopped
- Juice of 1 lime
- Salt and black pepper, to taste

For the Chicken:

- 4 boneless, skinless chicken breasts
- 2 tablespoons olive oil
- 1 teaspoon ground cumin
- 1 teaspoon chili powder
- 1/2 teaspoon garlic powder
- Salt and black pepper, to taste

Instructions:

Preheat your grill or grill pan over medium-high heat.
In a bowl, combine all the ingredients for the Mango Salsa – diced mango, finely chopped red onion, diced red bell pepper, chopped jalapeño, chopped cilantro, lime juice, salt, and black pepper. Mix well and set aside.
In a small bowl, mix olive oil, ground cumin, chili powder, garlic powder, salt, and black pepper to create a spice rub for the chicken.
Rub the spice mixture evenly over each chicken breast.
Grill the chicken breasts for approximately 6-8 minutes per side, or until the internal temperature reaches 165°F (74°C) and the chicken is cooked through.
Once the chicken is cooked, remove it from the grill and let it rest for a few minutes.
Serve the grilled chicken topped with the homemade Mango Salsa.

Enjoy this vibrant and flavorful Mango Salsa Chicken as a delicious and healthy meal!

Roasted Vegetable Quinoa Bowl

Ingredients:

For the Roasted Vegetables:

- 2 cups broccoli florets
- 1 bell pepper, thinly sliced
- 1 zucchini, sliced into rounds
- 1 carrot, sliced into thin strips
- 1 red onion, sliced
- 2 tablespoons olive oil
- 1 teaspoon dried thyme
- 1 teaspoon dried rosemary
- Salt and black pepper, to taste

For the Quinoa:

- 1 cup quinoa, rinsed
- 2 cups vegetable broth or water
- 1 tablespoon olive oil
- Salt, to taste

For the Tahini Dressing:

- 1/4 cup tahini
- 2 tablespoons lemon juice
- 1 tablespoon olive oil
- 1 clove garlic, minced
- Salt and black pepper, to taste
- Water, as needed to thin the dressing

Instructions:

Preheat your oven to 425°F (220°C).

In a large bowl, toss together broccoli florets, sliced bell pepper, zucchini rounds, carrot strips, and sliced red onion with olive oil, dried thyme, dried rosemary, salt, and black pepper.

Spread the seasoned vegetables on a baking sheet in a single layer.

Roast the vegetables in the preheated oven for 20-25 minutes or until they are tender and slightly caramelized, stirring halfway through the cooking time.

While the vegetables are roasting, prepare the quinoa. In a saucepan, combine rinsed quinoa and vegetable broth or water. Bring to a boil, then reduce heat to low, cover, and simmer for 15-20 minutes or until the quinoa is cooked and the liquid is absorbed.

Fluff the quinoa with a fork and stir in olive oil and salt.

In a small bowl, whisk together tahini, lemon juice, olive oil, minced garlic, salt, and black pepper. Add water as needed to achieve the desired consistency for the dressing.

Assemble the Quinoa Bowl:
- Divide the cooked quinoa among serving bowls.
- Top with the roasted vegetables.

Drizzle the Tahini Dressing over the quinoa and vegetables.

Garnish with fresh herbs or a sprinkle of sesame seeds if desired.

Serve the Roasted Vegetable Quinoa Bowl as a wholesome and satisfying meal. Enjoy the combination of nutritious quinoa, flavorful roasted vegetables, and creamy tahini dressing!

Grilled Portobello Mushrooms

Ingredients:

- 4 large portobello mushrooms, stems removed
- 3 tablespoons balsamic vinegar
- 2 tablespoons soy sauce or tamari (for a gluten-free option)
- 2 cloves garlic, minced
- 1 teaspoon dried thyme
- 1 teaspoon dried rosemary
- Salt and black pepper, to taste
- Olive oil (for brushing)

Instructions:

In a small bowl, whisk together balsamic vinegar, soy sauce or tamari, minced garlic, dried thyme, dried rosemary, salt, and black pepper to create the marinade.
Place the portobello mushrooms in a shallow dish, gill side up.
Brush the mushrooms generously with the marinade, ensuring it reaches the gills and covers the entire surface.
Let the mushrooms marinate for at least 15-20 minutes, allowing them to absorb the flavors.
Preheat your grill or grill pan over medium-high heat.
Brush the grill grates with a little olive oil to prevent sticking.
Place the marinated portobello mushrooms on the grill, gill side down.
Grill for 5-7 minutes per side, or until the mushrooms are tender and have nice grill marks.
Baste the mushrooms with any remaining marinade during grilling.
Once the mushrooms are cooked, remove them from the grill and serve immediately.
Optionally, drizzle with additional balsamic vinegar or a sprinkle of fresh herbs before serving.
Grilled Portobello Mushrooms can be enjoyed on their own, as a side dish, or as a topping for burgers or salads.
Enjoy the rich and savory flavor of these grilled portobello mushrooms!

Turkey and Vegetable Lettuce Wraps

Ingredients:

For the Turkey Filling:

- 1 lb ground turkey
- 1 tablespoon olive oil
- 1 onion, finely chopped
- 2 cloves garlic, minced
- 1 bell pepper, diced
- 1 zucchini, diced
- 1 carrot, grated
- 1 cup mushrooms, finely chopped
- 1 teaspoon ground cumin
- 1 teaspoon chili powder
- Salt and black pepper, to taste
- Fresh cilantro, chopped (for garnish)

For the Lettuce Wraps:

- Large lettuce leaves (such as iceberg or butter lettuce)

For the Sauce:

- 2 tablespoons soy sauce or tamari
- 1 tablespoon hoisin sauce
- 1 tablespoon rice vinegar
- 1 teaspoon sesame oil
- 1 teaspoon honey or maple syrup
- Sriracha or chili garlic sauce, to taste (optional)

Instructions:

In a large skillet, heat olive oil over medium-high heat.
Add chopped onion and minced garlic to the skillet. Sauté for 2-3 minutes until the onion becomes translucent.

Add ground turkey to the skillet and cook until browned, breaking it apart with a spoon.

Add diced bell pepper, diced zucchini, grated carrot, and chopped mushrooms to the skillet. Stir and cook for an additional 5-7 minutes until the vegetables are tender.

Season the turkey and vegetable mixture with ground cumin, chili powder, salt, and black pepper. Stir well to combine.

In a small bowl, whisk together soy sauce or tamari, hoisin sauce, rice vinegar, sesame oil, honey or maple syrup, and Sriracha or chili garlic sauce if using.

Pour the sauce over the turkey and vegetable mixture. Stir to coat evenly and cook for an additional 2-3 minutes.

Remove the skillet from heat and let the filling cool slightly.

To assemble the lettuce wraps, spoon the turkey and vegetable mixture onto large lettuce leaves.

Garnish with chopped fresh cilantro.

Serve the Turkey and Vegetable Lettuce Wraps immediately, and enjoy a flavorful and low-carb meal!

Optionally, you can add additional toppings such as sliced green onions, chopped peanuts, or a squeeze of lime juice.

Egg White Omelette with Spinach and Tomatoes

Ingredients:

- 4 large egg whites
- 1 cup fresh spinach, chopped
- 1/2 cup cherry tomatoes, halved
- 1/4 cup onion, finely chopped
- 1/4 cup bell pepper, diced (any color)
- 1 clove garlic, minced
- 1 tablespoon olive oil
- Salt and black pepper, to taste
- Fresh herbs (such as parsley or chives) for garnish (optional)

Instructions:

In a bowl, whisk the egg whites until frothy. Season with a pinch of salt and black pepper.
In a non-stick skillet, heat olive oil over medium heat.
Add chopped onion and diced bell pepper to the skillet. Sauté for 2-3 minutes until the vegetables start to soften.
Add minced garlic to the skillet and sauté for an additional 30 seconds until fragrant.
Add chopped spinach to the skillet and cook for 1-2 minutes, or until it wilts.
Pour the whisked egg whites into the skillet over the vegetables.
Allow the edges of the egg whites to set, then gently lift them with a spatula, letting the uncooked egg flow underneath.
Sprinkle halved cherry tomatoes over one half of the omelette.
Once the egg whites are mostly set but still slightly runny on top, carefully fold the omelette in half with a spatula.
Continue cooking for another 1-2 minutes, or until the omelette is cooked through.
Slide the Egg White Omelette with Spinach and Tomatoes onto a plate.
Garnish with fresh herbs if desired.
Serve immediately and enjoy a light and nutritious egg white omelette!

Note: Feel free to customize the omelette with your favorite herbs, cheese, or additional veggies for extra flavor.

Cucumber Avocado Salad

Ingredients:

- 2 large cucumbers, thinly sliced
- 2 ripe avocados, diced
- 1/4 cup red onion, thinly sliced
- 1/4 cup fresh cilantro, chopped
- 2 tablespoons extra-virgin olive oil
- 1 tablespoon lime juice
- Salt and black pepper, to taste
- Red pepper flakes (optional, for a bit of heat)

Instructions:

In a large bowl, combine thinly sliced cucumbers, diced avocados, sliced red onion, and chopped cilantro.

In a small bowl, whisk together extra-virgin olive oil and lime juice to create the dressing.

Pour the dressing over the cucumber, avocado, and onion mixture.

Gently toss the ingredients until well coated with the dressing.

Season the salad with salt and black pepper to taste. Adjust the seasoning as needed.

If you like a bit of heat, you can add red pepper flakes to the salad.

Let the Cucumber Avocado Salad sit for a few minutes to allow the flavors to meld.

Serve the salad as a refreshing and healthy side dish or enjoy it on its own.

This salad is best when served immediately to maintain the freshness of the ingredients.

Enjoy the crispness of cucumber, creaminess of avocado, and the burst of flavors in every bite!

Almond-Crusted Baked Chicken Tenders

Ingredients:

- 1 lb chicken tenders
- 1 cup almond flour
- 1 teaspoon garlic powder
- 1 teaspoon onion powder
- 1/2 teaspoon paprika
- 1/2 teaspoon dried thyme
- 1/2 teaspoon dried oregano
- Salt and black pepper, to taste
- 2 large eggs
- Cooking spray (olive oil or avocado oil)

Instructions:

Preheat your oven to 400°F (200°C). Line a baking sheet with parchment paper and lightly coat it with cooking spray.
In a shallow bowl, whisk together almond flour, garlic powder, onion powder, paprika, dried thyme, dried oregano, salt, and black pepper. This mixture will be the coating for the chicken tenders.
In another shallow bowl, beat the eggs.
Dip each chicken tender into the beaten eggs, ensuring it is fully coated.
Transfer the egg-coated chicken tender to the almond flour mixture, pressing the coating onto the chicken to adhere.
Place the coated chicken tender on the prepared baking sheet. Repeat the process for the remaining chicken tenders.
Lightly spray the top of the chicken tenders with cooking spray to promote browning.
Bake in the preheated oven for 15-18 minutes or until the chicken is cooked through and the coating is golden brown.
For an extra crispy texture, you can place the chicken tenders under the broiler for the last 1-2 minutes of cooking.
Remove the almond-crusted baked chicken tenders from the oven and let them rest for a few minutes.
Serve the chicken tenders with your favorite dipping sauce, such as mustard, tzatziki, or a low-carb ranch dressing.

Enjoy these delicious and healthier Almond-Crusted Baked Chicken Tenders as a satisfying snack or main dish!

Spinach and Feta Stuffed Chicken Breast

Ingredients:

- 4 boneless, skinless chicken breasts
- 2 cups fresh spinach, chopped
- 1/2 cup crumbled feta cheese
- 1/4 cup sun-dried tomatoes, chopped (optional)
- 2 cloves garlic, minced
- 1 tablespoon olive oil
- 1 teaspoon dried oregano
- 1 teaspoon dried thyme
- Salt and black pepper, to taste
- Toothpicks or kitchen twine (for securing)

Instructions:

Preheat your oven to 375°F (190°C).

In a skillet, heat olive oil over medium heat. Add minced garlic and sauté for about 1 minute until fragrant.

Add chopped spinach to the skillet and cook until wilted, about 2-3 minutes.

Remove the skillet from heat and stir in crumbled feta cheese and sun-dried tomatoes (if using). Season with dried oregano, dried thyme, salt, and black pepper. Mix well to combine.

Butterfly each chicken breast by making a horizontal cut through the center, being careful not to cut all the way through. Open the chicken breasts like a book.

Divide the spinach and feta mixture evenly among the opened chicken breasts, spreading it over one half of each breast.

Fold the other half of the chicken breast over the stuffing to enclose it. Secure the stuffed chicken breasts with toothpicks or kitchen twine.

Season the outside of the stuffed chicken breasts with a sprinkle of salt, pepper, and additional dried herbs if desired.

Place the stuffed chicken breasts in a baking dish.

Bake in the preheated oven for 25-30 minutes or until the chicken is cooked through and reaches an internal temperature of 165°F (74°C).

Remove the toothpicks or kitchen twine before serving.

Serve the Spinach and Feta Stuffed Chicken Breast with your favorite sides, such as roasted vegetables or a light salad.

Enjoy this flavorful and elegant stuffed chicken dish!

Lentil and Vegetable Soup

Ingredients:

- 1 cup dried green or brown lentils, rinsed and drained
- 1 onion, finely chopped
- 2 carrots, diced
- 2 celery stalks, diced
- 3 cloves garlic, minced
- 1 can (14 oz) diced tomatoes
- 6 cups vegetable broth
- 2 teaspoons ground cumin
- 1 teaspoon ground coriander
- 1 teaspoon smoked paprika
- 1 bay leaf
- Salt and black pepper, to taste
- 2 cups chopped kale or spinach
- 2 tablespoons olive oil
- Fresh parsley, chopped (for garnish)
- Lemon wedges (for serving)

Instructions:

In a large pot, heat olive oil over medium heat. Add chopped onion, diced carrots, and diced celery. Sauté for 5-7 minutes until the vegetables are softened.
Add minced garlic to the pot and sauté for an additional 1-2 minutes until fragrant.
Stir in ground cumin, ground coriander, and smoked paprika, coating the vegetables with the spices.
Add rinsed lentils, diced tomatoes (with their juices), vegetable broth, and a bay leaf to the pot. Season with salt and black pepper to taste.
Bring the soup to a boil, then reduce the heat to low, cover, and simmer for 25-30 minutes or until the lentils are tender.
Add chopped kale or spinach to the soup and cook for an additional 5 minutes until the greens are wilted.
Adjust the seasoning if needed and remove the bay leaf.

Ladle the Lentil and Vegetable Soup into bowls.
Garnish with fresh parsley and serve with lemon wedges on the side for a burst of freshness.
Enjoy this hearty and nutritious Lentil and Vegetable Soup as a comforting meal, especially on colder days!

Lemon Herb Baked Cod

Ingredients:

- 4 cod fillets
- 2 tablespoons olive oil
- 2 tablespoons fresh lemon juice
- 2 teaspoons Dijon mustard
- 2 cloves garlic, minced
- 1 teaspoon dried oregano
- 1 teaspoon dried thyme
- Salt and black pepper, to taste
- Lemon slices (for garnish)
- Fresh parsley, chopped (for garnish)

Instructions:

Preheat your oven to 400°F (200°C). Line a baking sheet with parchment paper or lightly grease it.

In a small bowl, whisk together olive oil, fresh lemon juice, Dijon mustard, minced garlic, dried oregano, dried thyme, salt, and black pepper.

Place the cod fillets on the prepared baking sheet.

Brush the cod fillets with the lemon-herb mixture, ensuring they are well coated on all sides.

Arrange lemon slices on top of each cod fillet for added flavor.

Bake in the preheated oven for 12-15 minutes or until the cod is cooked through and flakes easily with a fork.

If desired, broil the cod for an additional 2-3 minutes to get a golden brown color on top.

Remove the baked cod from the oven and garnish with fresh chopped parsley.

Serve the Lemon Herb Baked Cod with your favorite sides, such as steamed vegetables, quinoa, or a light salad.

Enjoy this light, flavorful, and healthy dish!

Roasted Sweet Potato Wedges

Ingredients:

- 2 large sweet potatoes, washed and cut into wedges
- 2 tablespoons olive oil
- 1 teaspoon smoked paprika
- 1 teaspoon ground cumin
- 1/2 teaspoon garlic powder
- 1/2 teaspoon onion powder
- 1/2 teaspoon dried thyme
- Salt and black pepper, to taste
- Fresh parsley, chopped (for garnish, optional)

Instructions:

Preheat your oven to 425°F (220°C). Line a baking sheet with parchment paper or lightly grease it.
In a large bowl, combine sweet potato wedges with olive oil, smoked paprika, ground cumin, garlic powder, onion powder, dried thyme, salt, and black pepper.
Toss until the sweet potato wedges are evenly coated with the seasoning.
Arrange the seasoned sweet potato wedges in a single layer on the prepared baking sheet.
Bake in the preheated oven for 25-30 minutes, flipping the wedges halfway through the cooking time, or until the sweet potatoes are tender and golden brown.
If you like your sweet potato wedges extra crispy, you can broil them for an additional 2-3 minutes at the end.
Remove the roasted sweet potato wedges from the oven and let them cool for a few minutes.
Garnish with fresh chopped parsley if desired.
Serve the Roasted Sweet Potato Wedges as a delicious and nutritious side dish.
Enjoy these flavorful sweet potato wedges on their own or with your favorite dipping sauce!

Greek Salad with Feta and Olives

Ingredients:

- 4 cups mixed salad greens (romaine, iceberg, or your choice)
- 1 cup cherry tomatoes, halved
- 1 cucumber, diced
- 1/2 red onion, thinly sliced
- 1/2 cup Kalamata olives, pitted
- 1/2 cup crumbled feta cheese
- 1/4 cup extra-virgin olive oil
- 2 tablespoons red wine vinegar
- 1 teaspoon dried oregano
- Salt and black pepper, to taste

Instructions:

In a large salad bowl, combine mixed salad greens, cherry tomatoes, diced cucumber, sliced red onion, Kalamata olives, and crumbled feta cheese.
In a small bowl or jar, whisk together extra-virgin olive oil, red wine vinegar, dried oregano, salt, and black pepper to create the dressing.
Drizzle the dressing over the salad and toss gently to coat the ingredients evenly.
Adjust the seasoning if needed and toss again.
Serve the Greek Salad with Feta and Olives immediately as a refreshing side dish or light lunch.
Optionally, garnish with additional feta cheese and olives.
Enjoy the vibrant flavors of this classic Greek salad with the combination of crisp vegetables, tangy feta, and briny olives!

Baked Eggplant Parmesan

Ingredients:

- 2 large eggplants, sliced into 1/2-inch rounds
- Salt, for sweating the eggplant
- 2 cups marinara sauce
- 2 cups shredded mozzarella cheese
- 1 cup grated Parmesan cheese
- 1 cup breadcrumbs (Italian seasoned, if available)
- 1/2 cup chopped fresh basil or parsley (for garnish)
- Olive oil, for brushing

Instructions:

Preheat your oven to 400°F (200°C).

Slice the eggplants into 1/2-inch rounds. Place the slices on a paper towel-lined baking sheet, sprinkle with salt, and let them sit for about 30 minutes. This helps draw out excess moisture and bitterness from the eggplant.

After 30 minutes, pat the eggplant slices dry with paper towels to remove excess moisture.

Brush each side of the eggplant slices with olive oil and place them on a baking sheet.

Bake the eggplant slices in the preheated oven for about 15-20 minutes or until they are tender and slightly golden. Flip the slices halfway through the baking time.

While the eggplant is baking, prepare the breadcrumb mixture. In a shallow bowl, combine breadcrumbs with grated Parmesan cheese.

In a separate baking dish, spread a thin layer of marinara sauce.

Once the eggplant slices are done baking, remove them from the oven. Dip each slice into the breadcrumb mixture, ensuring they are well-coated on both sides.

Place the breadcrumb-coated eggplant slices in the baking dish on top of the marinara sauce.

Spoon more marinara sauce on top of each eggplant slice, covering them evenly.

Sprinkle shredded mozzarella cheese over the eggplant slices.

Bake in the oven for an additional 20-25 minutes or until the cheese is melted and bubbly, and the edges are golden brown.

Remove from the oven and let it cool for a few minutes.

Garnish with chopped fresh basil or parsley before serving.
Serve the Baked Eggplant Parmesan as a delicious and comforting vegetarian dish.
Enjoy the layers of flavors in this classic Italian-inspired dish!

Shrimp and Broccoli Stir-Fry

Ingredients:

- 1 lb large shrimp, peeled and deveined
- 4 cups broccoli florets
- 2 tablespoons soy sauce
- 1 tablespoon oyster sauce
- 1 tablespoon hoisin sauce
- 1 tablespoon cornstarch
- 2 tablespoons water
- 2 tablespoons sesame oil
- 3 cloves garlic, minced
- 1 tablespoon fresh ginger, grated
- 2 tablespoons vegetable oil
- Cooked white rice, for serving
- Sesame seeds and sliced green onions, for garnish (optional)

Instructions:

In a small bowl, mix soy sauce, oyster sauce, hoisin sauce, cornstarch, and water to create the sauce. Set aside.
Heat vegetable oil in a wok or large skillet over medium-high heat.
Add minced garlic and grated ginger to the hot oil. Stir-fry for about 30 seconds until fragrant.
Add shrimp to the wok and cook for 2-3 minutes until they start to turn pink.
Add broccoli florets to the wok and continue stir-frying for an additional 3-4 minutes until the shrimp are fully cooked and the broccoli is crisp-tender.
Pour the prepared sauce over the shrimp and broccoli. Stir well to coat the ingredients evenly.
Drizzle sesame oil over the stir-fry and toss to combine.
Cook for an additional 2-3 minutes, allowing the sauce to thicken.
Remove the wok from heat.
Serve the Shrimp and Broccoli Stir-Fry over cooked white rice.
Garnish with sesame seeds and sliced green onions if desired.
Enjoy this quick and flavorful shrimp and broccoli stir-fry for a delicious and nutritious meal!

Quinoa-Stuffed Bell Peppers

Ingredients:

- 4 large bell peppers, halved and seeds removed
- 1 cup quinoa, rinsed and cooked according to package instructions
- 1 can (15 oz) black beans, drained and rinsed
- 1 cup corn kernels (fresh or frozen)
- 1 cup diced tomatoes
- 1 cup diced red onion
- 1 cup diced avocado
- 1 cup shredded cheddar or Mexican blend cheese
- 1/4 cup chopped fresh cilantro
- 1 teaspoon ground cumin
- 1 teaspoon chili powder
- Salt and black pepper, to taste
- Lime wedges, for serving

Instructions:

Preheat your oven to 375°F (190°C).
In a large bowl, combine cooked quinoa, black beans, corn, diced tomatoes, red onion, avocado, shredded cheese, chopped cilantro, ground cumin, and chili powder. Mix well.
Season the quinoa mixture with salt and black pepper to taste.
Place the halved bell peppers in a baking dish.
Spoon the quinoa mixture into each bell pepper half, pressing it down gently.
Cover the baking dish with aluminum foil.
Bake in the preheated oven for 25-30 minutes or until the bell peppers are tender.
Remove the foil and bake for an additional 5-10 minutes until the cheese on top is melted and bubbly.
Remove the Quinoa-Stuffed Bell Peppers from the oven.
Garnish with additional chopped cilantro and serve with lime wedges on the side.
Enjoy these colorful and nutritious quinoa-stuffed bell peppers as a satisfying and wholesome meal!

Caprese Salad with Fresh Mozzarella

Ingredients:

- 4 large tomatoes, sliced
- 1 pound fresh mozzarella cheese, sliced
- Fresh basil leaves
- Extra-virgin olive oil
- Balsamic glaze (optional)
- Salt and black pepper, to taste

Instructions:

Arrange the tomato and mozzarella slices on a serving platter, alternating them for a visually appealing presentation.
Tuck fresh basil leaves between the tomato and mozzarella slices.
Drizzle extra-virgin olive oil over the salad.
Optionally, drizzle balsamic glaze over the top for added sweetness and depth of flavor.
Season the Caprese salad with salt and black pepper to taste.
Serve immediately and enjoy this classic and refreshing Caprese Salad with Fresh Mozzarella as a delightful appetizer or side dish!

Baked Chicken Thighs with Rosemary

Ingredients:

- 4-6 bone-in, skin-on chicken thighs
- 2 tablespoons olive oil
- 2 tablespoons fresh rosemary, chopped
- 4 cloves garlic, minced
- 1 teaspoon paprika
- Salt and black pepper, to taste
- Lemon wedges (for serving, optional)

Instructions:

Preheat your oven to 400°F (200°C).
In a small bowl, mix together olive oil, chopped rosemary, minced garlic, paprika, salt, and black pepper to create a marinade.
Place the chicken thighs in a large bowl or a zip-top plastic bag.
Pour the marinade over the chicken thighs, ensuring they are well-coated. Massage the marinade into the chicken.
Cover the bowl or seal the bag and let the chicken marinate for at least 30 minutes, or refrigerate overnight for a more intense flavor.
Place the marinated chicken thighs on a baking sheet lined with parchment paper.
Bake in the preheated oven for 35-40 minutes or until the chicken thighs are cooked through, and the skin is golden and crispy.
If desired, broil the chicken for an additional 2-3 minutes to get a more golden brown color on top.
Remove from the oven and let the chicken rest for a few minutes before serving.
Serve the Baked Chicken Thighs with Rosemary with lemon wedges on the side for a burst of freshness.
Enjoy these flavorful and aromatic baked chicken thighs as a delicious main dish!

Avocado and Black Bean Salsa

Ingredients:

- 1 can (15 oz) black beans, drained and rinsed
- 2 avocados, diced
- 1 cup corn kernels (fresh, frozen, or canned)
- 1 cup cherry tomatoes, quartered
- 1/2 cup red onion, finely chopped
- 1/4 cup fresh cilantro, chopped
- 1 jalapeño, seeds removed and finely chopped (optional for heat)
- Juice of 2 limes
- 2 tablespoons extra-virgin olive oil
- Salt and black pepper, to taste
- Tortilla chips (for serving)

Instructions:

In a large bowl, combine black beans, diced avocados, corn kernels, quartered cherry tomatoes, finely chopped red onion, chopped cilantro, and chopped jalapeño (if using).
In a small bowl, whisk together lime juice and extra-virgin olive oil to create the dressing.
Pour the dressing over the avocado and black bean mixture. Gently toss to coat all the ingredients.
Season with salt and black pepper to taste. Adjust the seasoning if needed.
Cover the bowl and refrigerate the Avocado and Black Bean Salsa for at least 30 minutes to allow the flavors to meld.
Before serving, give the salsa a final gentle toss.
Serve with tortilla chips as a refreshing and flavorful appetizer or side dish.
Enjoy this Avocado and Black Bean Salsa as a tasty and healthy snack!

Lemon Basil Grilled Chicken

Ingredients:

- 4 boneless, skinless chicken breasts
- 2 tablespoons olive oil
- Zest of 1 lemon
- Juice of 2 lemons
- 3 tablespoons fresh basil, chopped
- 3 cloves garlic, minced
- Salt and black pepper, to taste
- Lemon slices (for garnish, optional)

Instructions:

Preheat your grill to medium-high heat.
In a small bowl, whisk together olive oil, lemon zest, lemon juice, chopped basil, minced garlic, salt, and black pepper to create the marinade.
Place the chicken breasts in a shallow dish or a zip-top plastic bag.
Pour the marinade over the chicken, ensuring each breast is well-coated.
Marinate for at least 30 minutes, or refrigerate for a few hours for more flavor.
Remove the chicken from the marinade and let any excess drip off.
Grill the chicken breasts on the preheated grill for 6-8 minutes per side, or until the internal temperature reaches 165°F (74°C) and the chicken is cooked through.
While grilling, baste the chicken with the leftover marinade to keep it moist and flavorful.
Remove the grilled Lemon Basil Chicken from the grill and let it rest for a few minutes.
Garnish with lemon slices if desired.
Serve the Lemon Basil Grilled Chicken as a delicious and light main dish.
Enjoy the bright and zesty flavors of this grilled chicken recipe!

Broccoli and Cauliflower Gratin

Ingredients:

- 1 head broccoli, cut into florets
- 1 head cauliflower, cut into florets
- 2 tablespoons butter
- 2 tablespoons all-purpose flour
- 2 cups milk
- 1 cup shredded cheddar cheese
- 1/2 cup grated Parmesan cheese
- Salt and black pepper, to taste
- 1/2 teaspoon garlic powder
- 1/4 teaspoon nutmeg
- 1 cup breadcrumbs
- Fresh parsley, chopped (for garnish, optional)

Instructions:

Preheat your oven to 375°F (190°C).
Bring a large pot of salted water to a boil. Add the broccoli and cauliflower florets and cook for 3-4 minutes until they are slightly tender. Drain and set aside.
In a saucepan over medium heat, melt the butter. Stir in the flour to create a roux and cook for 1-2 minutes until it becomes lightly golden.
Gradually whisk in the milk, ensuring there are no lumps. Continue to cook, stirring constantly, until the mixture thickens.
Reduce the heat to low and add the shredded cheddar cheese and grated Parmesan cheese. Stir until the cheese is melted and the sauce is smooth.
Season the cheese sauce with salt, black pepper, garlic powder, and nutmeg. Adjust the seasoning to taste.
In a large bowl, combine the blanched broccoli and cauliflower with the cheese sauce. Toss until the vegetables are well coated.
Transfer the mixture to a greased baking dish.
In a small bowl, mix the breadcrumbs with a little melted butter to moisten them. Sprinkle the buttered breadcrumbs evenly over the broccoli and cauliflower mixture.
Bake in the preheated oven for 25-30 minutes or until the top is golden brown, and the gratin is bubbling.

Remove from the oven and let it cool for a few minutes.
Garnish with chopped fresh parsley if desired.
Serve the Broccoli and Cauliflower Gratin as a delicious and comforting side dish.
Enjoy the creamy and cheesy goodness of this vegetable gratin!

Turkey and Vegetable Skewers

Ingredients:

- 1 lb turkey breast, cut into cubes
- 1 zucchini, sliced
- 1 bell pepper, cut into chunks
- 1 red onion, cut into wedges
- Cherry tomatoes
- 3 tablespoons olive oil
- 2 tablespoons balsamic vinegar
- 1 teaspoon dried oregano
- 1 teaspoon garlic powder
- Salt and black pepper, to taste
- Wooden skewers, soaked in water for 30 minutes

Instructions:

In a bowl, whisk together olive oil, balsamic vinegar, dried oregano, garlic powder, salt, and black pepper to create the marinade.
Place the turkey cubes in a shallow dish and pour half of the marinade over them. Toss to coat the turkey evenly. Let it marinate for at least 30 minutes.
In another bowl, toss the sliced zucchini, bell pepper chunks, red onion wedges, and cherry tomatoes with the remaining marinade.
Preheat your grill or grill pan to medium-high heat.
Thread the marinated turkey cubes and mixed vegetables alternately onto the soaked wooden skewers.
Grill the skewers for about 10-15 minutes, turning occasionally, until the turkey is cooked through and the vegetables are tender and slightly charred.
Remove the Turkey and Vegetable Skewers from the grill.
Serve them hot with your favorite side dishes or over a bed of rice.
Enjoy these flavorful and colorful turkey and vegetable skewers as a delicious and healthy meal!

Butternut Squash Soup

Ingredients:

- 1 medium-sized butternut squash, peeled, seeded, and diced
- 1 onion, chopped
- 2 carrots, peeled and chopped
- 2 apples, peeled, cored, and chopped
- 3 cloves garlic, minced
- 4 cups vegetable or chicken broth
- 1 teaspoon ground cinnamon
- 1/2 teaspoon ground nutmeg
- 1/4 teaspoon ground ginger
- Salt and black pepper, to taste
- 2 tablespoons olive oil
- 1 cup coconut milk (optional, for added creaminess)
- Fresh parsley or chives, chopped (for garnish)

Instructions:

In a large pot, heat olive oil over medium heat. Add chopped onions and garlic, sautéing until softened.
Add diced butternut squash, chopped carrots, and apples to the pot. Cook for 5-7 minutes, allowing the vegetables and apples to slightly caramelize.
Pour in the vegetable or chicken broth, ensuring it covers the vegetables. Bring the mixture to a boil.
Reduce the heat to low, cover the pot, and simmer for about 20-25 minutes or until the butternut squash is tender.
Using an immersion blender, blend the soup until smooth and creamy. If you don't have an immersion blender, carefully transfer the soup in batches to a blender and blend until smooth. Remember to let it cool slightly before blending.
Season the soup with ground cinnamon, ground nutmeg, ground ginger, salt, and black pepper. Adjust the seasoning to taste.
If desired, stir in coconut milk for added creaminess.
Simmer the soup for an additional 5-10 minutes to allow the flavors to meld.
Ladle the Butternut Squash Soup into bowls.
Garnish with fresh parsley or chives.
Serve this warm and comforting soup as an appetizer or a light meal.

Enjoy the delicious flavors of this butternut squash soup!

Blueberry and Almond Smoothie

Ingredients:

- 1 cup blueberries (fresh or frozen)
- 1 banana
- 1/2 cup almond milk
- 1/4 cup Greek yogurt
- 1 tablespoon almond butter
- 1 tablespoon chia seeds (optional)
- 1 teaspoon honey or maple syrup (optional, for added sweetness)
- Ice cubes (optional)

Instructions:

Place blueberries, banana, almond milk, Greek yogurt, almond butter, chia seeds (if using), and honey or maple syrup (if using) in a blender.
If you prefer a colder smoothie, add a handful of ice cubes to the blender.
Blend on high speed until the ingredients are well combined and the smoothie reaches your desired consistency.
Taste the smoothie and adjust the sweetness if necessary by adding more honey or maple syrup.
Pour the Blueberry and Almond Smoothie into a glass.
Garnish with additional blueberries or a sprinkle of sliced almonds if desired.
Serve immediately and enjoy this refreshing and nutritious smoothie!

Roasted Garlic Hummus

Ingredients:

- 1 can (15 oz) chickpeas, drained and rinsed
- 1/4 cup tahini
- 1/4 cup extra-virgin olive oil, plus more for drizzling
- 2 tablespoons lemon juice
- 3 cloves roasted garlic
- 1/2 teaspoon ground cumin
- Salt, to taste
- Water (as needed to adjust consistency)
- Paprika (for garnish)

Instructions:

Preheat your oven to 400°F (200°C).

Cut the top off a head of garlic to expose the cloves. Drizzle the garlic head with olive oil and wrap it in aluminum foil. Roast in the preheated oven for 30-40 minutes or until the garlic cloves are soft and golden.

In a food processor, combine chickpeas, tahini, olive oil, lemon juice, roasted garlic cloves, ground cumin, and a pinch of salt.

Blend the ingredients until smooth and creamy. If the hummus is too thick, add water, one tablespoon at a time, until you reach your desired consistency.

Taste the hummus and adjust the seasoning by adding more salt or lemon juice if needed.

Transfer the Roasted Garlic Hummus to a serving bowl.

Drizzle with extra-virgin olive oil and sprinkle with paprika for garnish.

Serve the hummus with pita bread, vegetable sticks, or your favorite crackers.

Enjoy this delicious and flavorful Roasted Garlic Hummus as a tasty dip or spread!

Chickpea and Spinach Curry

Ingredients:

- 2 tablespoons olive oil
- 1 large onion, finely chopped
- 3 cloves garlic, minced
- 1 tablespoon ginger, grated
- 1 tablespoon curry powder
- 1 teaspoon ground cumin
- 1 teaspoon ground coriander
- 1/2 teaspoon turmeric
- 1/2 teaspoon cayenne pepper (adjust to taste)
- 1 can (15 oz) chickpeas, drained and rinsed
- 1 can (14 oz) diced tomatoes
- 1 can (14 oz) coconut milk
- 4 cups fresh spinach leaves
- Salt and black pepper, to taste
- Fresh cilantro, chopped (for garnish, optional)
- Cooked rice or naan bread (for serving)

Instructions:

In a large skillet or pan, heat olive oil over medium heat.
Add chopped onions and sauté until they become translucent.
Stir in minced garlic and grated ginger. Cook for an additional 1-2 minutes until fragrant.
Add curry powder, ground cumin, ground coriander, turmeric, and cayenne pepper to the onion mixture. Stir well to coat the onions with the spices.
Add the drained chickpeas to the skillet and cook for 2-3 minutes, allowing them to absorb the flavors.
Pour in the diced tomatoes with their juices and the coconut milk. Stir to combine all the ingredients.
Bring the mixture to a simmer, then reduce the heat to low and let it simmer for about 15-20 minutes, stirring occasionally.
Add fresh spinach leaves to the curry and cook until they wilt.
Season the Chickpea and Spinach Curry with salt and black pepper to taste.
Adjust the seasoning as needed.
Serve the curry over cooked rice or with naan bread.

Garnish with chopped fresh cilantro if desired.
Enjoy this hearty and flavorful Chickpea and Spinach Curry as a delicious vegetarian meal!

Balsamic Glazed Salmon

Ingredients:

- 4 salmon fillets
- Salt and black pepper, to taste
- 2 tablespoons olive oil
- 1/4 cup balsamic vinegar
- 2 tablespoons honey
- 2 cloves garlic, minced
- 1 teaspoon Dijon mustard
- Fresh parsley, chopped (for garnish)

Instructions:

Preheat your oven to 400°F (200°C).
Season the salmon fillets with salt and black pepper.
In an oven-safe skillet, heat olive oil over medium-high heat.
Place the salmon fillets in the skillet, skin-side down, and sear for 2-3 minutes until the skin becomes crispy.
Flip the salmon fillets using a spatula, and transfer the skillet to the preheated oven.
Bake the salmon for 10-12 minutes or until the salmon is cooked through and flakes easily with a fork.
While the salmon is baking, prepare the balsamic glaze. In a small saucepan, combine balsamic vinegar, honey, minced garlic, and Dijon mustard. Bring the mixture to a simmer and cook for 3-4 minutes until it thickens slightly.
Once the salmon is cooked, remove the skillet from the oven.
Drizzle the balsamic glaze over the salmon fillets.
Garnish with chopped fresh parsley.
Serve the Balsamic Glazed Salmon hot, either on its own or with your favorite side dishes.
Enjoy this simple and flavorful salmon dish with a delightful balsamic glaze!

Watermelon and Feta Salad

Ingredients:

- 4 cups cubed seedless watermelon
- 1 cup crumbled feta cheese
- 1/2 cup fresh mint leaves, chopped
- 2 tablespoons extra-virgin olive oil
- 1 tablespoon balsamic glaze or balsamic reduction
- Salt and black pepper, to taste

Instructions:

In a large serving bowl, combine the cubed watermelon, crumbled feta cheese, and chopped fresh mint leaves.
Drizzle the extra-virgin olive oil over the salad.
Season the salad with salt and black pepper to taste.
Gently toss the ingredients to coat the watermelon and feta with the olive oil and seasonings.
Drizzle balsamic glaze or balsamic reduction over the Watermelon and Feta Salad for a sweet and tangy finish.
Toss the salad again to evenly distribute the balsamic glaze.
Refrigerate the salad for 15-30 minutes to allow the flavors to meld and the salad to chill.
Before serving, give the Watermelon and Feta Salad a final gentle toss.
Serve the refreshing and colorful salad as a side dish or a light summer appetizer.
Enjoy the sweet and savory combination of watermelon and feta with a burst of freshness from mint!

Turkey and Quinoa Meatballs

Ingredients:

- 1 lb ground turkey
- 1 cup cooked quinoa, cooled
- 1/2 cup breadcrumbs
- 1/4 cup grated Parmesan cheese
- 1/4 cup chopped fresh parsley
- 1 egg
- 2 cloves garlic, minced
- 1 teaspoon dried oregano
- 1 teaspoon dried basil
- 1/2 teaspoon onion powder
- Salt and black pepper, to taste
- Olive oil (for greasing or cooking spray)

Instructions:

Preheat your oven to 375°F (190°C). Grease a baking sheet with olive oil or use a cooking spray.
In a large mixing bowl, combine ground turkey, cooked quinoa, breadcrumbs, grated Parmesan cheese, chopped fresh parsley, egg, minced garlic, dried oregano, dried basil, onion powder, salt, and black pepper.
Mix the ingredients until well combined. Be careful not to overmix.
With damp hands, form the mixture into meatballs of your desired size and place them on the prepared baking sheet.
Bake the Turkey and Quinoa Meatballs in the preheated oven for 20-25 minutes or until they are cooked through and have reached an internal temperature of 165°F (74°C).
Optional: If you want to brown the meatballs slightly, you can broil them for an additional 2-3 minutes.
Remove the meatballs from the oven and let them rest for a few minutes.
Serve the Turkey and Quinoa Meatballs with your favorite sauce, pasta, or as appetizers.
Enjoy these flavorful and protein-packed meatballs as a wholesome and nutritious meal!

Spaghetti Squash with Tomato Sauce

Ingredients:

- 1 medium-sized spaghetti squash
- 2 tablespoons olive oil
- 2 cloves garlic, minced
- 1 can (14 oz) crushed tomatoes
- 1 teaspoon dried oregano
- 1 teaspoon dried basil
- 1/2 teaspoon red pepper flakes (optional, for heat)
- Salt and black pepper, to taste
- Fresh basil, chopped (for garnish)
- Grated Parmesan cheese (optional, for serving)

Instructions:

Preheat your oven to 400°F (200°C).
Cut the spaghetti squash in half lengthwise. Scoop out the seeds and fibers.
Drizzle the cut sides of the spaghetti squash with olive oil and season with salt and black pepper.
Place the spaghetti squash halves, cut side down, on a baking sheet.
Roast the spaghetti squash in the preheated oven for 40-45 minutes or until the flesh is tender and easily pierced with a fork.
While the spaghetti squash is roasting, prepare the tomato sauce. In a saucepan, heat olive oil over medium heat.
Add minced garlic and sauté for about 1 minute until fragrant.
Pour in the crushed tomatoes and add dried oregano, dried basil, red pepper flakes (if using), salt, and black pepper. Stir to combine.
Simmer the tomato sauce for 15-20 minutes, allowing the flavors to meld and the sauce to thicken. Adjust the seasoning as needed.
Once the spaghetti squash is done, use a fork to scrape the flesh into spaghetti-like strands.
Serve the spaghetti squash with the tomato sauce on top.
Garnish with chopped fresh basil and, if desired, grated Parmesan cheese.
Enjoy this low-carb and gluten-free Spaghetti Squash with Tomato Sauce as a healthy and satisfying alternative to traditional pasta dishes!

Green Bean Almondine

Ingredients:

- 1 lb fresh green beans, trimmed
- 2 tablespoons olive oil
- 2 tablespoons sliced almonds
- 2 cloves garlic, minced
- 1 tablespoon lemon juice
- Salt and black pepper, to taste
- Fresh parsley, chopped (for garnish)

Instructions:

Bring a large pot of salted water to a boil. Add the trimmed green beans and cook for 2-3 minutes, or until they are bright green and slightly tender. Drain the green beans and immediately transfer them to a bowl of ice water to stop the cooking process. Drain again and set aside.
In a large skillet, heat olive oil over medium heat.
Add sliced almonds to the skillet and toast them for 1-2 minutes, stirring frequently until they become golden brown. Be cautious not to burn the almonds.
Add minced garlic to the skillet and sauté for about 30 seconds until it becomes fragrant.
Add the blanched green beans to the skillet and toss them with the almond and garlic mixture.
Drizzle lemon juice over the green beans and continue to cook for an additional 2-3 minutes, or until the green beans are heated through.
Season the Green Bean Almondine with salt and black pepper to taste. Toss to combine.
Transfer the green beans to a serving dish.
Garnish with chopped fresh parsley.
Serve immediately as a delicious and vibrant side dish.
Enjoy the crisp and flavorful Green Bean Almondine!

Berry Chia Seed Pudding

Ingredients:

- 1/2 cup chia seeds
- 2 cups almond milk (or any plant-based milk)
- 1 teaspoon vanilla extract
- 1 tablespoon maple syrup or agave syrup (adjust to taste)
- Mixed berries (strawberries, blueberries, raspberries) for topping
- Optional: Sliced almonds or coconut flakes for garnish

Instructions:

In a bowl, combine chia seeds, almond milk, vanilla extract, and maple syrup. Stir well to combine.

Cover the bowl and refrigerate the chia seed mixture for at least 2 hours or overnight, allowing it to thicken. Stir the mixture a few times during the first hour to prevent clumping.

After the chia pudding has reached a pudding-like consistency, give it a good stir. Spoon the chia seed pudding into serving glasses or bowls.

Top the pudding with mixed berries and, if desired, garnish with sliced almonds or coconut flakes.

Serve the Berry Chia Seed Pudding immediately or refrigerate until ready to serve. Enjoy this healthy and delicious chia seed pudding as a satisfying breakfast or snack!

Grilled Vegetable Kabobs

Ingredients:

- 1 zucchini, sliced
- 1 yellow bell pepper, cut into chunks
- 1 red bell pepper, cut into chunks
- 1 red onion, cut into chunks
- 1 cup cherry tomatoes
- 8-10 button mushrooms
- 2 tablespoons olive oil
- 2 cloves garlic, minced
- 1 teaspoon dried oregano
- 1 teaspoon dried thyme
- Salt and black pepper, to taste
- Wooden or metal skewers

Instructions:

If using wooden skewers, soak them in water for at least 30 minutes to prevent burning.
Preheat the grill to medium-high heat.
In a bowl, combine olive oil, minced garlic, dried oregano, dried thyme, salt, and black pepper. Mix well to create the marinade.
Thread the vegetables onto the skewers, alternating between different vegetables for a colorful presentation.
Brush the vegetable kabobs with the prepared marinade, ensuring they are well-coated.
Place the vegetable skewers on the preheated grill.
Grill the kabobs for about 10-15 minutes, turning occasionally, or until the vegetables are tender and have grill marks.
Remove the grilled vegetable kabobs from the grill and transfer them to a serving plate.
Optional: Drizzle extra olive oil and sprinkle additional herbs for added flavor.
Serve the Grilled Vegetable Kabobs as a delicious and healthy side dish or main course.
Enjoy the vibrant and smoky flavors of these grilled vegetables!

Coconut Flour Banana Pancakes

Ingredients:

- 2 ripe bananas, mashed
- 4 large eggs
- 1/4 cup coconut flour
- 1/2 teaspoon baking powder
- 1/2 teaspoon vanilla extract
- Pinch of salt
- Coconut oil or butter for cooking
- Optional toppings: sliced bananas, berries, maple syrup

Instructions:

In a mixing bowl, combine mashed bananas, eggs, coconut flour, baking powder, vanilla extract, and a pinch of salt. Stir well until the batter is smooth.
Let the batter sit for a few minutes to allow the coconut flour to absorb the liquid and thicken.
Heat a skillet or griddle over medium heat and add a small amount of coconut oil or butter.
Scoop about 1/4 cup of the batter onto the hot skillet to form each pancake.
Cook the pancakes for 2-3 minutes on one side until bubbles form on the surface. Flip the pancakes and cook for an additional 1-2 minutes on the other side, or until golden brown.
Repeat the process with the remaining batter.
Serve the Coconut Flour Banana Pancakes with your favorite toppings, such as sliced bananas, berries, or a drizzle of maple syrup.
Enjoy these delicious and gluten-free pancakes for a nutritious breakfast!

Lemon Dijon Grilled Chicken

Ingredients:

- 4 boneless, skinless chicken breasts
- Zest and juice of 1 lemon
- 3 tablespoons Dijon mustard
- 2 tablespoons olive oil
- 2 cloves garlic, minced
- 1 teaspoon dried thyme
- Salt and black pepper, to taste
- Fresh parsley, chopped (for garnish)

Instructions:

In a bowl, whisk together lemon zest, lemon juice, Dijon mustard, olive oil, minced garlic, dried thyme, salt, and black pepper to create the marinade.
Place the chicken breasts in a resealable plastic bag or a shallow dish.
Pour the marinade over the chicken, making sure each piece is well-coated. Seal the bag or cover the dish, and refrigerate for at least 30 minutes to allow the flavors to infuse.
Preheat the grill to medium-high heat.
Remove the chicken from the marinade and let any excess drip off.
Grill the chicken breasts for 6-8 minutes per side, or until they are cooked through and have nice grill marks. The internal temperature should reach 165°F (74°C).
Remove the grilled chicken from the heat and let it rest for a few minutes.
Garnish with chopped fresh parsley.
Serve the Lemon Dijon Grilled Chicken with your favorite side dishes.
Enjoy this flavorful and zesty grilled chicken as a delicious and healthy meal!

Greek Tzatziki Sauce

Ingredients:

- 1 cup Greek yogurt
- 1 cucumber, finely grated
- 2 cloves garlic, minced
- 1 tablespoon extra-virgin olive oil
- 1 tablespoon fresh lemon juice
- 1 tablespoon fresh dill, chopped
- Salt and black pepper, to taste

Instructions:

Start by grating the cucumber using a fine grater. Place the grated cucumber in a clean kitchen towel and squeeze out the excess liquid.
In a bowl, combine the Greek yogurt, grated cucumber, minced garlic, extra-virgin olive oil, fresh lemon juice, and chopped dill.
Mix the ingredients thoroughly until well combined.
Season the Tzatziki sauce with salt and black pepper to taste. Stir again.
Cover the bowl with plastic wrap and refrigerate for at least 1-2 hours to allow the flavors to meld.
Before serving, give the Tzatziki sauce a final stir.
Taste and adjust the seasoning if needed.
Serve the Greek Tzatziki Sauce as a refreshing and tangy condiment for gyros, grilled meats, or as a dip for veggies.
Enjoy the authentic flavors of this classic Greek sauce!

Mixed Berry Smoothie Bowl

Ingredients:

- 1 cup mixed berries (strawberries, blueberries, raspberries)
- 1 frozen banana, sliced
- 1/2 cup Greek yogurt
- 1/4 cup almond milk (or any plant-based milk)
- 1 tablespoon honey or maple syrup (optional, for sweetness)
- Toppings: sliced strawberries, blueberries, granola, chia seeds, shredded coconut

Instructions:

In a blender, combine the mixed berries, frozen banana slices, Greek yogurt, almond milk, and honey or maple syrup.

Blend the ingredients until smooth and creamy. If needed, add more almond milk to reach your desired consistency.

Pour the smoothie into a bowl.

Top the Mixed Berry Smoothie Bowl with sliced strawberries, blueberries, granola, chia seeds, and shredded coconut.

Customize the toppings based on your preferences.

Serve immediately and enjoy this vibrant and nutritious smoothie bowl for a refreshing breakfast or snack!

www.ingramcontent.com/pod-product-compliance
Lightning Source LLC
LaVergne TN
LVHW081619060526
838201LV00054B/2323